Temptation

Tom L. Eisenman

InterVarsity Press
P.O. Box 1400, Downers Grove, IL 60515
World Wide Web: www.ivpress.com
E-mail: mail@ivpress.com

InterVarsity Press is the book-publishing division of InterVarsity Christian Fellowship/USA, a student movement active on campus at hundreds of universities, colleges and schools of nursing in the United States of America, and a member movement of the International Fellowship of Evangelical Students. For information about local and regional activities, write Public Relations Dept., InterVarsity Christian Fellowship/USA, 6400 Schroeder Rd., P.O. Box 7895, Madison, WI 53707-7895.

ISBN 0-87784-058-X

Printed in the United States of America ∞

16	15	14	13	12	11	10	9	8	7	6	5	4	3	2
12	11	10	09	08	07	06	05	04	03	02	01			

It is amazing to me how a temptation can come seemingly out of nowhere and gain power in my life. Since I've written and taught on this topic for years, a person would think I'd have it all down by now and not be bothered by these troublesome temptations anymore. But it is still necessary, as the apostle Peter says, to "be self-controlled and alert. Your enemy the devil prowls around like a roaring lion looking for someone to devour" (1 Pet 5:8).

My wife, Judie, and I were on a trip recently when someone stole my golf clubs. I had been wish-dreaming for some time about getting better clubs, hoping they would improve my game. Now I had no clubs at all. When I contacted our insurance company, I found that our deductible was about equal to the value of my clubs. I would get nothing from turning in a claim.

That's when I was hit with the temptation. *Just tell the insurance company you had more expensive clubs. Build up the retail cost of the clubs, the bag, the shoes, the balls, the whole thing.* The idea grew in me. Fortunately the Lord intervened before I acted on my bad idea. Pretty soon every time I tried to pray about anything, the image of new golf clubs and a ripped-off insurance company would come into my head. The Lord made it abundantly clear to me that there was no way I could lie about my loss without utterly destroying my prayer life.

At the same time I was about to preach a sermon on the topic of righteous living. As I prepared, the reality came home to me: *I am actually playing with the idea of turning in a false insurance claim!* I could not stand in front of my congregation and preach to them on making good and righteous choices in their lives while I was considering such a bad choice in mine. The following Sunday I closed the message with a confession about how tempted I had been to turn in a falsified claim.

There is power in bringing our struggles and temptations to the light. Once I shared it openly, the temptation vanished. It is a great feeling to be free!

Remember Who You Are

My golf club incident is a success story. God kept me from the sins of lying and stealing. There have been many other times when I have not let God have his way and I've failed him. When this happens it is easy to get discouraged and feel defeated. That's why it is important to remember who we are as believers.

By faith in Jesus Christ we stand forgiven and have been welcomed into God's forever family. We are children of God (1 Jn 3:1). We are at different levels of maturity in the process of allowing Christ's likeness to be formed in us (Gal 4:19). We are not yet fully what we will be when we see Jesus face to face, but that doesn't mean that we are not in the family. It just means that we have some growing up to do.

We may at times have long-term struggles with temptation and sin. But the struggles we experience do not mean God has given up on us. The fact that we experience tension when we think about acting against God's will is assurance that God is really very close to us. If we did not belong to him, we could sin without feeling remorse. The struggle is proof of who we are.

We will all lose many battles in our attempts to live the holy life. That's why we need a Savior. When we fail, God stands ready to forgive (1 Jn 1:8-10). The most important thing is that we keep getting up again and again, willing to step back into the fight. Proverbs 24:16 says, "Though a righteous man falls seven times, he rises again."

Take hold of the promise the apostle Paul gives us in Philippians 1:6: "He who began a good work in you will carry it on to completion until the day of Christ Jesus." God is at work in your life! By the power of the Holy Spirit, Christ is being formed in you. It will take a lifetime for him to complete his work. But do not lose heart. God keeps his promises.

The Temptation Process

As we mature in Christ, we learn how to cooperate with the Holy Spirit as God completes his work in us. The rest of this booklet is designed to help you better understand the temptation process and learn some practical strategies for resisting temptation before it leads you into sinful choices that impede your progress with God.

James writes, "But each one is tempted when, by his own evil desire, he is dragged away and enticed. Then, after desire has conceived, it gives birth to sin; and sin, when it is full-grown, gives birth to death" (Jas 1:14-15).

James says temptation begins in the mind as the product of a connection between our inner desires and some object in the world. Desire is conceived in the mind, and sin is born when we act on our evil desire. Sin that is full-grown brings forth death. The wages of sin is always death, Romans 6:23 tells us. If sin is allowed to grow in our lives, it will destroy us.

Most often it takes little more than our selfish needs or desires and what the world offers to make tempting situations difficult to resist. But James wants to show us one more element that powerfully influences the temptation process. Jesus is not the only fisher of men. James believes there is an evil fisherman at work in our lives who can both create and energize connections between our selfish desires and the world. This evil one's motivation is never to catch and release.

James's use of fishing imagery makes this point. The one who is tempted is "dragged away and enticed." We are hungry. We see the bait. We are lured by it. Finally we bite. We are netted, hooked, taken in tow by our desires. Then we are dragged away. Anytime we give in to temptation, our relationship with God suffers. We need to find ways to stop the progress of temptation before it leads us into continued sin.

What we want as children in the family of God is to be able to echo Paul's testimony before his death, "I have fought the good fight, I have finished the race, I have kept the faith" (2 Tim 4:7). This is a *battle* we are in. It is not easy to fight the good fight. But God is more than able to build tenacious character into our lives if we are willing to be built. We can be men and women of strength and courage who have what it takes to wrestle against temptations that threaten to erode our character and cripple the witness of the church.

Here are seven practical and helpful strategies for staying in the fight.

Strategy 1: Know Yourself
The prophet Jeremiah says, "The heart is

deceitful above all things and beyond cure. Who can understand it?" (Jer 17:9).

One of the major stumbling blocks to our progress against sin is simply our inability quickly and easily to identify and admit our weaknesses. It takes courage to admit to God and others that we do not have it all together in our Christian lives. But this admission is absolutely necessary before God can begin his work in any area where we need to grow.

Make a study of your vulnerable areas. Pray that God will reveal to you those things that you think, do or say that cause harm to yourself, others or your relationship with God. What in your life has power to lead you away from God? Is it alcohol? pornography? vanity? gossip? Do you hold grudges? Do you struggle with prayerlessness? Take note of the areas of vulnerability you and God have to work on. That's a good start!

Pray also that God will show you the deeper needs underlying your typical temptations. Sometimes we try to deal with issues without understanding that they are simply symptoms of a deeper problem. God can and will lead you to greater awareness and understanding of yourself that will help you find legitimate and healthy ways to get your real needs met.

Make a study too of your vulnerable times and the recurring patterns of certain temptations that gain ground in your life. I know, for instance, that I am more vulnerable to temptation when I am exhausted. Fatigue reduces my will power and opens me up for all kinds of things I would normally be able to resist. Knowing this helps. If I need sleep and rest, I have to choose to take time for myself—otherwise I can expect to encounter temptation.

Perhaps you are weaker when you've been disappointed by something or somebody. Or you reach for comforts when you are depressed or lonely. Knowing our vulnerable times can help us to create defenses to protect ourselves from being led down a path that will only compound our problems.

Strategy 2: Seek Renewal in the Spirit

New spiritual life always comes from a work of the Holy Spirit that begins with authentic repentance. Acts 3:19 says, "Repent, then, and turn to God, so that your sins may be wiped out, that times of refreshing may come from the Lord." Second Corinthians 7:10 talks about the power of "godly sorrow" operating in us to lead us to new life. We are never closer to joy than when our hearts earnestly cry out for God's mercy and forgiveness.

Godly sorrow leads to heartfelt repentance. Repentance is a turning toward God and away from sin. As we choose obedience, the Lord's refreshing floods in. We seal these steps toward obedience with accountability. James says, "Therefore, confess your sins to each other and pray for each other so that you may be healed." Whenever I find myself struggling in an area and experiencing difficulty in moving to freedom, I know that I must bring this temptation or sin into the open if I am serious about growing past it.

The principle I believe to be absolutely biblical and powerful to change our lives is this: *Renewal begins in repentance, continues in obedience, strengthened by accountability.* If we apply this truth to areas of sin and struggle, we will be different people.

I have made a covenant with God about sexual purity when I travel alone, stay in hotels and speak to groups. In my life without God I developed a vulnerability to sexually explicit materials like those offered today on hotel pay-per-view channels. My sorrow regarding this led me to repentance many years ago. I also determined that I would create a strategy to help me remain obedient in this area.

The first thing I do when I go into a hotel room is find the code on the remote that removes the pay-per-view channels from the TV. I do that while I am still fresh and alert. The next thing I do is take out all my family pictures and stand them up on the dresser so I have my whole family staring at me, reminding me who I am. But before I even leave home I take Judie's hand in mine and say, "I want to be the same person when I'm away from you as I am right now, standing here with you, holding your hand. Ask me if I've been faithful in this when I come home." She always prays for me, and on my return she asks me how things went.

Renewal will happen regularly in our Christian lives if we live in the context of a strong faith, exposing ourselves continually to the things of God. We need to be regular in worship. We need to be in relationship with God in prayer. We need to be studying the Bible. As we know God more and more through his Word, we are less likely to be deceived about who he is and what he is able to accomplish in our lives.

Strategy 3: Know Your Enemy

The Bible teaches that there is a devil, and that his agenda is to oppose God's work in every area of our lives. The evil one is clever and crafty, deceitful and a liar (Gen 3:1; Acts 13:10; Jn 8:44). It is important to understand how Satan works in our lives to lead us away from God and his purposes for us.

Satan's strategy is typified by his work with Eve in the beginning to bring about the original sin. God had commanded Adam and Eve not to eat the fruit from the tree in the center of the garden. Enter the serpent. He engages Eve in a discussion that calls God's command into question: "Did God really say, 'You must not eat from any tree in the garden'?" (Gen 3:1).

At this point Eve makes the fatal mistake. She and Adam have been given authority over all the creatures in the garden (Gen 1:26). Eve's response should have been, "You have no authority to speak to me about things that concern Adam, me and God." But she stumbles, submitting her authority to the serpent, and he takes control.

The next step for the serpent is to place doubt in Eve's mind about the truth of what

God has said. Eve tells the serpent she and Adam are not to eat of the fruit or they will die. He tells her, "You will not surely die. For God knows that when you eat of it your eyes will be opened, and you will be like God" (vv. 4-5). In two brief sentences the serpent has called God a liar—pictured God as jealous and protective of his position.

Now Eve begins to think that the curse would really be a blessing. She is attracted to the appearance of the fruit, and she is sure it will be delicious, but above all, she now becomes convinced that it is what she needs to become everything she can be. Eve acts. She eats. She becomes the devil's advocate. She offers the fruit to Adam. He eats. The Fall is complete.

The first thing Satan will try is to engage us in dialogue about sin and create doubt about what God may have really said or meant, or about whether God really has our best interests in mind. "Did God really say . . . ?" His strategy is to give our minds ample opportunity to form doubt or rationalization, and to connect some craving we have with an attractive but off-limits object, thought or experience.

It is impossible to beat Satan in a debate, so don't try. Our best response is always to drive the dialogue out of our minds, to choose to talk to God instead. Refuse to discuss it. Break it off. Otherwise you will suddenly find yourself thinking crazy thoughts, such as that something you know is against God's will for you may really be exactly what you need to fulfill your life. How can we be so foolish as to think that something good can ever come from something evil?

Temptation begins in the mind. We have to be careful who we give our minds to. Satan will take the gifts God has given us and use them to his own advantage. Our creative imagination, for instance, is given to us by God so that we can hold the vision of who we are in Christ and who we can become by the power of God. But the evil one perverts the gift. We find ourselves fantasizing instead about some sin, playing with tempting ideas in our minds. When we act on these evil imaginings, we find that the experience in reality is only a pale shadow of what we held in our minds. We also do not consider the consequences of our behavior, the ugly feelings that invade after we have sinned and the destructiveness of these acts to our relationship with God and others. Tricked again.

Another clever maneuver of Satan is to give us the most powerful experience of some sin at the front end. Most sinful behaviors have elements of pleasure or excitement in them. As we act we are exhilarated by our self-assertion. But the devil does this to trap us. From that point on we will only experience a rapidly increasing appetite for a steadily decreasing pleasure.

You have authority from Christ over the evil one. Say directly to the devil, "You have no authority to talk with me about things that concern God and me." That's what Jesus was doing when he repeatedly responded to

Satan's suggestions to him in the wilderness with the phrase "It is written" (Mt 4). He used God's Word to defend himself against Satan's seductive powers. Involve God immediately in a situation when you are tempted. When the evil one comes knocking at your door, just say, "God, would you get that?"

Strategy 4: Live with a Vision

Living with a vision can be a powerful motivating factor for resisting temptation. Without a vision to live up to we will live at the level of what the world around us is accepting and promoting. Having and holding a vision from God for our lives will help us to swim upstream in our downstream world.

Paul writes in Romans 12:2, "Do not conform any longer to the pattern of this world, but be transformed by the renewing of your mind." As we continually study God's Word, our minds are revitalized by the truth of his promises. Understanding our position in Christ fortifies our minds against the constant barrage of the world's ideas. If we instead conform our minds and lives to the attitude of the world, we will always give in too soon, without a fight, and we will be smaller people than God wants us to be. Don't let the world tell you who you are, how you're supposed to think and act, or what values are important. Look to God and his Word for a vision.

This is not just to strengthen yourself. The world today desperately needs men and women who can lead others out of the present mire of moral confusion and decay. It is important to realize that we cannot lead anyone further than we ourselves have walked in faith. Our challenge is to be always ready to take that next step with the Lord. If we are growing in Christ, we will become visionary leaders, God's ambassadors who carry with us in every situation a passionate, God-guided, transforming vision for our hurting world.

Strategy 5: Develop Good Habits

A habit is a predisposition to act in a predictable manner each time a certain set of circumstances arises. We all have good and bad habits. Good habits are disciplines we build into our lives through repeatedly acting in healthy and appropriate ways. Good habits are our best intentions trained for action.

Bad habits are formed through neglect. We simply do the wrong thing consistently and repeatedly and form a bad habit. Proverbs 25:28 says, "A weak man is like a city broken into and left without walls." A lack of disciplined development of good habits leaves us defenseless, easily overcome. As the blocks crumble in one area of our walls of defense, usually before long another area begins to give way as well. Soon we find that things which used to bother our Christian consciences no longer make us feel uncomfortable. Then we are in real danger.

Forming good habits is like adding building blocks to the walls of defense that surround and protect us. These good habits make godly responses automatic. We don't want to have to think about what we should do when a tempting set of circumstances arises. We want to be able simply to act appropriately. Forming a good habit will do this for us. And as we take one area under control, it becomes easier to address another area with success. Soon we are strong cities, fortified with walls of defense.

Remember, a good habit is as hard to break as a bad habit.

Strategy 6: Beware of Your Strengths

This may sound strange when we've been talking all along about how to build strength against temptation, but sometimes we may just *think* we are strong in some area when really we have just not been tested. The apostle Paul writes, "So, if you think you are standing firm, be careful that you don't fall" (1 Cor 10:12).

A close friend of mine, a deeply committed Christian woman, shared with me a surprising experience she had at a Christian conference. She is married to a Christian man, but they have struggled in their relationship. Nevertheless she is absolutely committed to her marriage. Being tempted to involve herself with another man would have been the farthest thing from her mind.

On the first morning of the conference my friend found herself being particularly responsive to one of the married men in her small group. He had pain in his life similar to some of the marital pains she had gone through. This man also had many of the winsome qualities she had always hoped would be present in her husband but weren't.

The two of them had lunch together, and dinner later. At the end of the evening he walked her back to her hotel room. It was not until the moment they stood together in the hallway outside her room that she realized the full extent of what was happening. A situation she would have thought impossible twenty-four hours earlier was now a very real and powerful temptation.

They said good night and parted. The next day they changed groups and did not see each other again. They won that battle.

Be careful about the areas in your life that you feel are your strong areas. Perhaps you have not been fully tested there. The Chinese proverb is true: "It is on the path you do not fear that the wild beast catches you."

The other thing about our strengths is that they have dark sides. It is usually in an area of strength or giftedness that we will be tempted to use our ability to gain something for ourselves, manipulating others to fulfill some private, ungodly agenda. Just ask yourself what your strengths are and how you might be tempted to use your strengths and gifts in choices that would not be pleasing to God. This is a good defensive strategy that will yield results in your life.

Strategy 7: Run from Temptation

A Greek term used often by New Testament writers to challenge us in the area of temptation is *pheugō*. The word simply means "run away" or "flee." An effective defense we have against temptation is to run away from it.

"Flee from sexual immorality" (1 Cor 6:18); "flee from idolatry" (1 Cor 10:14); "flee the evil desires of youth, and pursue righteousness, faith, love and peace, along with those who call on the Lord out of a pure heart" (2 Tim 2:2). James adds that if we will run away from sin and turn to God, then the devil will run away from us: "Submit yourselves, then, to God. Resist the devil and he will flee from you" (Jas 4:7).

The Old Testament story of Joseph and Potiphar's wife, found in Genesis 39, is an example of resisting temptation by fleeing. Joseph was skilled in management, and Potiphar entrusted his property and household to Joseph's care. Everything went well for a while. Although Potiphar's wife wanted Joseph to sleep with her, he continually resisted this temptation.

Potiphar was away from the property one day, and Joseph was in the house. Potiphar's wife grabbed Joseph by the cloak, saying,

"Come to bed with me!" Joseph ran out of the house leaving his cloak behind. It was the right response.

We need to develop a similar decisiveness about attitudes, experiences, thoughts and things that tempt us. Whenever one of these starts to control you, run from it—physically or mentally—and to a Scripture passage that will help you maintain balance. You may want to ask a mature Christian friend to pray with you about this area of temptation in your life. This is how you run from temptation, whether you struggle with anger or addictions or prejudices or profanity.

It takes courage to run. Running from a temptation is not a cowardly thing at all but rather a sign of maturity in Christ. Mature Christians know their limits and how to act decisively to protect themselves. Running is simply one more important way to take action and get tough with temptation.

Taking action in an external way does not immediately change the inner needs and desires that make us vulnerable, nor does it banish the recurrent situation that brings about the temptation. But when our courageous and decisive action is accompanied by an authentic repentance and a deep desire to be made new, taking a bold first step to run from the temptation can go a long way toward freedom and lasting victory in this troublesome area of your life.

We have a marvelous scriptural promise in 1 Corinthians 10:13: "No temptation has seized you except what is common to man. And God is faithful; he will not let you be tempted beyond what you can bear. But when you are tempted, he will also provide a way out so that you can stand up under it." We need to be more courageous fighters, both battling against each temptation and running away from it, all the way to the door of escape that God provides.

I believe we can actually learn to enjoy this fight, growing to love dethroning and putting to death in our lives the things that exert their twisted power over us. Each time we are willing to take the fight to the limit—and we find out God is faithful in his promise to provide a door of escape—our faith, strength and courage advance by a quantum leap.

Why Do We Fight This Fight?

Jesus said, "If you obey my commands, you will remain in my love, just as I have obeyed my Father's commands and remain in his love. I have told you this so that my joy may be in you and that your joy may be complete" (Jn 15:10-11).

The Lord's goal for our lives is that we have joy and live in joy. When sin has wedged its way into our lives, it colors everything gray. We live a clouded existence. We cannot freely and comfortably relate to those around us when sin is in our lives. Even though Jesus stands ready to forgive, our repeated confessions can leave us feeling like failures. God wants us to be free. He wants us to experience victory through the power of the Holy Spirit who lives in us and strengthens us for this battle (Rom 8:3-4).

As important as it is to God that we experience personal freedom, peace and joy, there is more. We are also to positively influence the world around us (Mt 5:13-14). On one level this has to do with our witness to the world as members of Christ's church. When temptation creates a lack of confidence and focus in our lives, the resulting instability makes it difficult for us to get outside our own problems and give ourselves in love to others (Jas 1:8). But we can show the world that it is possible to make progress and to be a different people by the power of God working in and through us (Eph 3:20-21).

We have a responsibility to our children, our families, our Christian brothers and sisters—to the world around us—to show that our lives can truly be changed forever by the power of Christ. Let's be men and women who model for the next generation that it is possible to make the tough decisions and live a courageously clean life in the Lord. Jesus wants to build that in us, his church. Are you willing to be built into the mature character of Christ?

One final thought. The apostle Paul writes in Ephesians 3:10-11 that God's intention is "that now, through the church, the manifold wisdom of God would be made known to the rulers and authorities in the heavenly realms, according to his eternal purpose which he accomplished in Christ Jesus our Lord." Our battle against temptation and sin is demonstrating to "rulers and authorities in the heavenly realms" what God is accomplishing in our world through the power of the cross of Christ.

Angels and devils alike are watching. Jesus told Peter, "Satan has asked to sift you as wheat. I have prayed for you, Simon, that your faith may not fail. And when you have turned back, strengthen your brothers" (Lk 22:31-32). Satan wants to sift our lives as well. Will we stand in faith, or will we fall?

We are God's examples of what the power of the resurrection can do in a believer's life.

We are being watched. Let's be living proof—
even to the spiritual forces of good and evil in
the universe—of the adequacy of the resurrection power of God in Christ to make us a people who, when temptation comes, stand firm.

---

*Tom Eisenman is a popular conference speaker and
the senior pastor at Chapel in the Pines in Arnold,
California. His books include* Temptations Men
Face *and* Temptations Families Face. *To con-
tact him about this booklet or possible speaking
engagements, e-mail him at <teisenman@ivpress.com>
or write him c/o InterVarsity Press, P.O. Box 1400,
Downers Grove, IL 60515.*